The
Drum-roll
in the Dark

David Bell Nicholson

Cowslip

Published by Cowslip Press

Cowslip

9 Casson Street
Ulverston
LA12 7JQ

First Published in 2019.

Designed and set by Russell Holden
Pixel Tweaks, Ulverston.
www.pixeltweakspublications.com

Cover illustration of Spindle Fruit by David Bell Nicholson

ISBN: 978-1-9996097-2-6

For our family and friends.

Acknowledgements

I am deeply indebted to Caroline Gilfillan for her commitment to this endeavour. She responded wholeheartedly to the task of editing – considerable, as David left many versions of each poem – to the setting up all that is necessary to produce a coherent and sympathetic collection and to publishing it through her recently established Cowslip Press.

I would like to thank Margaret and Peter Whyte and Kim Moore for their critiques and for the encouragement and affection they always gave to David.

Further acknowledgement must go to the National Galleries of Scotland, for its *Inspired. Get Writing!* competition, in which David was placed second as an unpublished poet. Also to Liz Nuttall, Kerry Darbishire and Kim Moore for their inclusion of David's poem in Handstand Press's recently published Cumbrian anthology, *This Place I Know*.

The friendships of Liz and Gordon Nuttall, Jenny and Martin Copley, Margaret and Peter Whyte, Barrow Writers, the A Poem and a Pint committee, Ross and Josie Baxter and Ina Anderson were central in David's life. For this I thank them. Finally I want to thank Pat and Peter Marsden for their constant interest, for the conviviality and conversations that we shared and for their on-going friendship and support.

Biography

David Bell Nicholson was born in Ulverston, Cumbria, in 1943, the youngest of three boys in a family that would be devastated by the loss of their father in 1951. This premature death came, in part, as a result of injuries received in WWI. David's mother was impoverished, a fact that taught him how gleaning, gathering and doing odd jobs were tagged onto schooling as a part of life. Very soon he was re-modelled in speech and behaviour and, though failing the 11+, at thirteen shot to the top of the A stream at Ulverston Grammar School and then to teacher training in Art and English at Chester College.

After experience in a Liverpool secondary modern school, where he also ran a boys' club, David chose to teach children with significant behavioural problems. His insight made him immensely skilled and successful as a class teacher and then as Deputy Head in a residential special school.

Aged 38 David suffered a heart attack, which meant surgery followed by full time retirement. This he weathered with considerable difficulty and fortitude. He ran the household, gardened and cooked for his teenage children and held his now extended family together. In his volunteer work supporting stroke victims and in Sure Start, his insights were key. In 1989 ill health became an ever-present factor but it was also the beginning of a period of intense poetry writing, reading, gardening and travel.

David was very sociable, cooking delicious suppers for his many friends. He had an unending store of jokes – always surprising with a new one. He died of a heart attack on December 19th 2013 with just one of his poems published.

Foreword

David's poems were written from 1981 onwards. Soon he and I began to share editing suggestions. Because he worked on his poems endlessly there are different versions from which I, finally, had to select for this collection.

He seldom submitted work for publication in magazines or for competitions, though the one exception, of which he was very proud, was The National Galleries of Scotland's *Inspired. Get Writing*, in which he was placed second as an unpublished poet. He joined Barrow Writers, but rarely went to workshops such was his diffidence. But as time went on and his health deteriorated, his childhood memories, his attachment to Cumbria, to nature and his garden, as well as his search for a philosophy of life, became preoccupations. With time and considerable soul searching, poetry became more and more his vehicle for understanding and expressing his thoughts and feelings. I have tried to reflect this in arranging these poems.

Gill Nicholson. Spring 2019

CONTENTS

The Five Lakes Tour 2

A Long Stand, High Carley Hospital. 4

Strawberries 5

Distemper... 6

WORLD WAR I AFTERSHOCKS 8

  1. Secrets 8

  2. Trajectory... 9

  3. Paper Seller.. 10

  4. White Lies... 11

  5. November 11/11 12

The Smooth Green Hill 14

1952-2012 A Change of Fortune............................. 15

Ned Cockerton 17

Maran Cockerel 18

Budgie 20

A Raleigh with a Sturmey-Archer Hub. 22

Woman in White 1964 23

Purity.. 24

Caliban Gets to The Grammar................................. 26

Indian Mynah Bird.. 27

Daffodillies 28

Co-habitation 29

Word Soccer 14th February 30

Reversion to Type.. 31

Henry's Daydream 32

Henry's Sunday...33

Henry Gardening...34

Kate and Henry's Private Garden 35

Henry and the Closed Drawer 36

Echo Location 38

Bullfinches 39

Begetting 40

Nor his Ox 40

Larkin' in the Long Grass. 42

Notice..43

You Are So Sincere...44

Earthworks in Edinburgh 45

Vitrine 48

Shore Leave with Sirens 50

A Day of Life..51

To Whom do You Talk when
You're Awake in the Night? 52

In This Interpretation of Events 53

Waking 54

The Ultimate Tram...55

Paranoia 57

Black Letter Days 58

– saving for a rainy day –

The Five Lakes Tour

Take care of pennies and the pounds'll
take care of themselves, my mam said.
I did. I saved them all:
trailed the coal-horse every Tuesday,
bread-horse every day
a bucket clanking on my shins.
I shovelled up the khaki nuggets
sold them for a ha'penny
to Mr Dixon down the street
who'd dug up cobbles in his yard
growing rhubarb and an orange rose
against the whitewashed lavvy wall.
I bet the rent-man didn't know.

Mondays I collected tatie peelings
door-to-door, an odd cabbage stalk
kept back by neighbours for my bucket.
Against the rules Mrs. Towers
had six hens in her back yard.
To make a mash she boiled
my peelings with some bran.
She gave me tuppence – not an egg.

A fool and his money are soon parted,
my mam said. On the top shelf
in the cupboard by the fire
I kept my slotted moneybox,
hinged base screwed tightly down.
At first it rattled, then grew heavy
with copper as I sold pounds
of blackbums to the corner shop
and rose hips, to be sent away
to make syrup for posh kids
with tickly coughs. Best of all
a silver thruppence given by my Uncle Dick
drunk in town on market day –
Don't tell your Aunty Lizzie, mind.

Mam had booked the Five Lakes Tour
with Hadwin's charabanc. She found
she couldn't pay for it, so steely eyed
she used the blunt end of a knife
to open up my money-box.
Twelve pennies to a pile, it added up
to seventeen and six – *enough*
to give your Dad a holiday.

Though born near Coniston, and four years
in Flanders, in all his life he'd never
seen Rydal Water or Grasmere.
He never did!
The rain – it never stopped;
the clouds – they never lifted.
My dad in trilby, not his cap,
my mother in white gloves,
sat side-by-side, us in front
to clout when fratchin'.
The windows ran with steam.
I studied how the drops would gather,
how the engine's shuddering would
send them racing down the glass.

We made our entertainment in those days.
But *saving for a rainy day*
just makes me laugh.

A Long Stand, High Carley Hospital.

A heap of horse-muck on the drive,
Mr Wilson forks it onto roses by the gates.
He drives the ambulance –
one day might take me home again.

He straightens up, rubs his back,
reaches for his jacket with the silver buttons on,
asks me, yes, asks me,
will I watch the heap till he comes back,
just in case some bugger tries to pinch a bit.

I stand tall as a sentry,
feet together, hands to sides
in my fever-red pyjama top.
Clicking his heels, he salutes me.

He's away for ages.
When he gets back, he shakes his head
and laughs a lot and calls me daft.
But how could I desert my post
when he has trusted me?

Strawberries

The pattern on the bedroom wall
began to crawl. A bogeyman
was crouching by the wardrobe door.
I tried to think about the smoothness
of the shell I'd found, traced
its spiral to a silent point.

When I woke I saw my brother
holding up my tadpole jar,
hundreds of strawberries from the quarry,
bright red in the tea-time sun.
It must have taken ages –
he'd not scoffed one.

He'd crossed the mad bull's field.
When it sniffed you in the air
it couldn't see to charge –
a bit of tractor mudguard
fastened to its horns
masked its eyes.

Mam complained at sugar from the ration
and a drop of milk she couldn't spare.
On my cracked and swollen tongue
the strawberries were sweeter
than I've ever tasted in my life.
I wish I'd told my brother this.

Distemper

I'm by the bedroom window
spying into next-door's garden.
They're having a funeral for a rabbit,
the parents holding their kids,
encouraging them to cry.

When I was that boy's age
my pup Laddie died.
On the hearthrug we'd laugh
into each others' eyes.
Then he got distemper –
the name of the sickly yellow paint
Mam daubed on the kitchen walls.

No explanation. No tears allowed.
Dad put him in a sack
and tied it to his bike handlebars.
When he got back home
there was red soil on the tyres.
He'd thrown Laddie in the clay-dubs.
Mam looked hard at me:
shut up and say nowt.

When Dad died we weren't allowed to cry.
Sometimes she'd set his place at table,
then remember. She didn't sob,
but we got our own tea those nights.
My best friend was killed by a bus
on his paper round. I didn't feel a thing.

Now I understand my parents more.
Dad had seen pals in Flanders
drown in shell holes.
He'd wrapped men up
and buried them in mud and quicklime.
His body was scarred by shrapnel,
his mind by nightmares.
Their lives were hard.
Lamenting didn't help.

My life is easy.
I can shrug my shoulders.
But last week I saw
a goldfish in a bowl
circle and circle a plastic castle
and I was unmanned.

WORLD WAR I AFTERSHOCKS

1. Secrets

My first tooth bloody in my hand
I run into their room.
It's Sunday morning,
Dad's in bed puffing on his pipe.
Sparks burn neat holes in the quilt.
My mother smiles her gleaming smile,
above me a St. Bruno-fragrant heaven.

Sunday next, toothache again.
She is alone, screwed up in bed.
It's getting light. Her mouth's a cave.
In a glass bright bubbles form
on pink false teeth I've never seen before.
I dare not wake her.
Dad is underneath the bed.

He's hidden by a grey gas-cape
his army boots a hollow for his head.
He whimpers like a dreaming dog.
They never told that after thirty years
whizz-bangs came screaming
all the way from Vimy Ridge
to burst inside his head.

2. Trajectory

In 1784 Henry Shrapnel invented a cannonball filled with lead shot as an anti-personnel weapon. During the Great War exploding shells were extensively used on the Western Front. The word shrapnel was used correctly for the contents but also for the shards or splinters of casing, which pierced the body.

I'd watched him washing after work
bending at the kitchen sink.
I'd pulled his dangling braces,
seen the holes between his ribs,
silver streaks across his back.
He'd turned and laughed at me, his *li'le lass*.

August Monday we were picking blackberries.
My father fell, barbs clutching at his Sunday suit.
Get someone. Get someone,
my mother screamed.
Leave the basket.
My sister ran.
I held Dad's trilby with red hands.

That day a shrapnel fragment stirred
and stopped my father's heart.

3. Paper Seller

He wore a leather helmet
like Sir Malcolm Campbell,
but his conveyance was a bogey cart
dogs peed against.

He pushed and pulled on levers
to crawl along the pavement.
I wished that I could have a go.

Where his bottom half was missing
Evening Mails were stacked.
I asked my mother how he used the lav.
She frowned and pushed me on.

He joked with all his customers,
passing up their change
though peoples' crotches
rubbed his nose in it.

4. White Lies

His left trouser leg was folded all the way and safety-pinned.
It was safer to study his crutches,
how the wood was polished by his hands,
how shiny the brass tacks and leather where his armpits rubbed.

After my dad died he turned up every Thursday,
a dewdrop dripping from his long blue nose.
He brought birds-of-paradise to show us,
copied in poster colour on the back of wallpaper.

My mother knitted gloves for him,
grey wool unravelled from a pullover.
He unrolled his gift for her.

Even I knew not to scrub the paper with the brush.
It's beautiful, she said,
but she threw it on the fire as soon as he had gone.

5. November 11/11

Seen on TV

that time when an ancient man
is wheeled out once more –
the last one who fought at Vimy Ridge.

He's asked about his pals.
I wonder if he knew my Dad –
search the glitter in his tortoise eyes.

Finally, there's a message on the screen:
Four days after this interview, Jack died.

I hadn't known my father
could be made more dead.

– a black-edged empty shape –

The Smooth Green Hill

The only picture in our house
Dad discovered in a rusty trunk.
It showed the parish church
in pen and ink and faded water paint.

Dad cut glass, made a frame and hung it
over the mantle shelf above the range.
He went and studied graves
to find and add the date.

At teatime, sunshine lit a couple arm-in-arm
in bonnet and top-hat, yews half their present size
and boys in britches fishing in a tarn
where now the Comprehensive stands.

Hardest to believe, the smooth green hill behind
had no lighthouse monument on top.

Yet often I had climbed the hill, traced Valentines
scratched in the monument's limestone wall.
I'd run around its base, hold out my coat
and lean against the gales from off the bay.

When Dad died suddenly, the vicar came.
He stood beside the hearth and sympathised
until Mam howled into her pinafore.
He praised the painting so effusively she gave it him.

He bounced off down the lobby,
duty done; left us with
a black-edged empty shape
to stare at on the chimney-breast.

1952-2012 A Change of Fortune.

Miss Wren told us that the King had died – we should all be very, very sad and pray for Princess Elizabeth. Two weeks earlier my Dad had died. Nobody said a word about that – just *Nicholson – free* when the dinner register was called. The rows in front turned round to stare. I felt hot.

The *Free* table was by the pig bin. A big lad kicked me on the shins. He had scabs, bruises and red cracked hands. The boy next to me smelled like a rabbit hutch. He stirred his dinner up and ate it with a spoon. Mam searched each night for biddies, scraping with a fine toothcomb and dusted me with DDT she used for killing cockroaches. I told her then I wanted to come home for dinners. She threw her purse down, gaping, empty on the table.

When they didn't need it for the fire, as an act of kindness, next-door dropped yesterday's Chronicle over the backyard wall. I wolfed down every word, escaping Mam's misery for a while. I saw Prince Charles in a velvet-collared coat sitting in his pedal car, his mother and his father smiling down. On the middle page he wore a kilt and knee socks with tabs; turrets towered over a massive lawn. One day I'd have a garden. In the meantime I made a castle from a cardboard box and stuck Prince Charles onto the front. His lugs made perfect targets for the dart I'd picked up outside The Rose and Crown.

For the Coronation, next-door got a television on the never-never – the first in our street. Mam sniffed: *with money like that I'd rent a house that isn't damp and has an inside lav.* They took the chairs away to fit more neighbours in. Even sitting on the floor in front, the screen was fuzzy. I liked the horse-guards, not the wizard holding up the crown.

Back home I asked Mam what all those Lords in ermine and Ladies with tiaras would be having for their teas, remembering jelly and custard in the Spritualists' Room on V.E. Day. *Peacocks' tongues in aspic I expect, but for a treat I'm making chips. No butties though, never mind what they do next door.*

I've bought my own Balmoral now, three-bed, c.h, detached, on Nob Hill. No moat but a bit of garden all around. Most of my friends are middle-class. Some were even born that way. They try to tell me that in the sixties they felt stigmatised for talking posh. I'll serve them delicious Coronation Chicken for the Jubilee. Such meat is shamefully cheap. We'll joke about whether it's U or Non-U now that kitsch is chic. We're all tossers. I'll tell them Camilla sent apologies, His and Hers, and a little box of Highgrove bics as well – perfect with the sherry trifle we're having for our afters.

In spite of herself, my mother would be proud of me.

Ned Cockerton

At dusk and dawn Ned pedalled,
legs akimbo, through the streets,
hooking gas lights up and down.
He wobbled round, one-handed,
shouldering the pole.

Foremost he was a poacher,
used his skills between
his duties lighting lamps
in those hungry years
selling rabbits to the magistrate.

One morning, before breakfast,
I was sent to dig for dandelions
to ease my Dad's lumbago.
The streets were barely aired,
crows flew from damp cobbles.

Ned was coming off the fell
his rough-haired lurcher at his heel.
It might have winked at me
but didn't dare. Bright grass
poked from Ned's coat pocket.

I wondered what was cradled there,
peewits' eggs, curlews' or gulls'?
But seeing black tobacco
dribbling down his bristly chin,
I didn't dare to ask.

Shyly I said
What dus ta feed tha dog on, Maister?
Stick n' watter, lad,
nobbut stick and watter
n'if it catches nowt,
it gits nae watter.

Maran Cockerel

The farm was built on bedrock,
yard worn smooth by centuries of clogs.
Marigolds shone by the lime-washed wall.
Her daddy helped his lass to sow the seed.
He'd covered them in mesh to keep the hens away,
big birds, her Mammy's pride –
a dozen speckled black Marans
eggs brown as bracken off the banks.

The menace was the cockerel –
fuck it or fight it was his creed.
He raped the hens and chased the cat,
the collie bitch skulked in the shippon door.
He'd mount the midden, scarlet comb erect
his wattles bright with blood.
Stretching up, he'd flap his wings
and crow and crow.

He fought the washing just for fluttering,
flew at it feet first, raked it with his spurs,
ripped the lass's knickers off the line –
and she was terrified.
Her mammy bawled at her for being nesh,
shoved her out across the yard
with peelings for the sow.
Against the pigsty stoop he cornered her.

He whirred his wings, pinions a hand of blades.
She cringed and shrieked and called,
hair ribbon dangling loose before her eyes.
Her daddy, chopping kindling, heard,
swore *I'll do yon bugger once 'n' fer all.*
He ran, axe in hand –
his hobnails skidding under him,
skull thudded on the rock.

In the days he took to die
the girl was stopped from seeing him.
Blood clots in 'is 'eed, she overheard
in angry whispering; didn't dare to say a word
feared the rough edge
of her mammy's tongue.
The funeral took place without her there –
her daddy gone like snow from off a dyke.

The marigolds are black with autumn rain.
The daughter runs away from Mammy's clouts –
I'll gi' thee summat t' bleat about –
hides among the boulders in the rough.
Late blackberries are full of worms.
She picks them, makes a mash,
squeezes pulp in red-stained hands;
dark drops gutter down the rocks.

Budgie

Joey's what they call him.
He hopes he's still a pretty boy.
His mirror lies hidden in husks
at the bottom of his cage.
Their mam used to brush them up
before she lost her man.

But now the mound of shit
has reached his perch.
His swing won't swing.
Her eldest wants to clean him out.
His mam clouts him and cries,
but still she doesn't do it.

She used to bath her bairns
beside the fire each Friday night.
He was set free to balance on the tub.
They made a lather with their hands,
blew bubbles in the air for him.
There's doubt these days that he can fly.

She set their daddy's place today
and then remembered –
threw her pinny over her head,
dropped into her chair.
The lads are getting their own tea:
butties with banana slices.

They don't look at his empty plate
or at each other; cut the loaf straight,
leave some for the morning,
spread marge thin.
The youngest nicks more sugar.
His brothers don't split on him.

Their mammy rocks and moans
like a ghost under a shroud.
Joey is fed up, decides to break the mood,
chirrups: *Hey I'm still alive.*
The big lad gets up,
drapes the tea cloth on his cage.

A Raleigh with a Sturmey-Archer Hub.

Me and my mate Billy
climbed up the quarry,
nicked a baby jackdaw from its nest.
What a racket all the others made.

Billy fed Jack bits of bread and worms.
It learnt to fly, came back each time
to perch on his shoulder,
hardly ever shitting down his back.

Billy got a paper round
to pay the never-never
for the bike to do the job:
a Raleigh with a Sturmey-Archer hub.

Jack flew behind,
caught up at halts,
took off again when Billy speeded up.
The bike was almost paid for

when Billy was killed – crushed
underneath the bobbin workers' bus,
just too soon
to get his Christmas tips.

When I heard, I hoped to get his bike
but it was wrecked,
even the bell.
I never saw Jack again.

Woman in White 1964

A neighbour sent a message to the college,
said his ma was near the end.
It took two days to reach him in the pub.
He hitched back home to see her,
found the coffin in the parlour –
so no reconciliation then.

Someone must have found her teeth.
She looked less bitter than she had for years
with roses in her filled-out cheeks,
approachable and happy – not disgraced by him,
not demented by her husband's death.
He felt her presence in the absence, but
what weakened Joe was bridal lace
like soft white doilies round her face.

Purity

Joe's aunty pined to marry Dicky Valentine.
Dressed all in white she waited after every show:
white pumps, white stockings and a white bouquet.
Joe's shoes stuck onto her carpets, polished
bright as lino – years of dog shit trodden in.
She loved her strays, must have dressed for Dicky
in a public lav to be so clean and pure for him.

– looking for the pearls –

Caliban Gets to The Grammar

After fifty years he's visiting his English teacher.
She still wears that corset-coloured lipstick,
her mouth is not like satin any more.
He's looking for the pearls that were her nails
but her hand above the sheet is waxy green;
there's a smell of seaweed in the ward.

Yes, Nicholson, it's you – I remember –
you gave me your poem
'A White Raft of Gulls.'
At fourteen he was full of piss and passion
for ripe metaphor. She'd opened
his cloth lugs and freckled pores
to sounds and sweet airs.

After class, with lowered eyes, she told him
he could sign up for the Stratford trip
and pay at half-a-crown a week.
Next dinnertime he stayed behind,
brought the first instalment
from his wood-cutting wage.

He pressed against the table where she sat.
Sunshine lit the powdered down on her top lip.
She put his cash in a tobacco tin –
Parson's Pleasure, Mild, Ready Rubbed.
Pointing, he said, *I'd rather have*
a Strong Rough Shag myself.

Her mouth twitched; quietly she said,
When I lift the lid the smell
reminds me of my husband's pipe.
He guessed a cardigan and tartan slippers,
gazed at her with moon-calf eyes.
She wouldn't look at him, neither did she
move her small hand from the table-top.
Chalk dust hung on the hot still air.

Indian Mynah Bird

At Conishead Priory, on the shore of Morecambe Bay
a hundred miles south-west of the Durham collieries,
there was a miners' convalescent home.

Gunga Din would listen for those lads,
the ones with wind enough
who'd struggle up the street
thirsty for The Farmers Arms.
At the rattle of the latch
he'd cock his head,
his eyes bright, yellow beak agape.

He'd shake his dusky feathers out,
leap around from perch to perch:
Haway, canny lads, he'd crow.
Us boozers always laughed.
The Durham fellas grinned,
gasped: *Haway spuggy marra,*
from their coal-caked lungs.

When the men were gone
who'd dug as far beneath the waves
as Bardsea is from Morecambe –
rocks and sands and all that weight
of water overhead –
the home closed down.

Yet still the locals risked a smile
as Gunga hacked and hawked
and asked: *What are yer 'avin pet?*
and called the bar-maid Bonny Lass
and coughed and coughed as if
his breast were clagged with dust.

Daffodillies

In Cumbrian dialect daffodils are called lillies. Here, Wordsworth's poem is mocked by a local who finds To Daffodils an irritating eulogy. He wants to smash their heads off.

Ay up! Weer's me stick?

I's gang t'bray t'eeds reet off them lillies,
'sides t'watter, nunder yon trees,
girt lock o'em, year atter year, 'arrishin' me.

I's telt I mun "conserve their habitat,"
mind 'em fer "future generations,"
gay thrang, all t'damn same.

Lookster! I's unique like –
an' think on, so's thou –
'til tha's deed.

An' nae mair 'an folk's 'membrin'.
Li'le bits o'soot 'n shite
'ave nowt t'be pensive wi'; 'appen vacant mebbe.

Sithee, thar's nobbut yan o'me
n'I's fair moidered wi't lillies gangin' on
ferivver'n' ivver a ditherin' n'a dancin'.

Bliss o'solitude? My arse!
Sod t'couch. Gi'us me stick.
Let's awa t't pub!

Co-habitation

She pleads to keep her room her own.
He craves to share his room with her
begs her to unbolt his door
open his window, enjoy his view,
a meal, a joke, his comfy bed.

She fears he'll cross her threshold,
unsettle her pine bench with cushions,
ask her what she thinks about,
scrawl his thoughts upon her walls,
swallow her whole with his eyes.

Word Soccer 14th February

We play the word association game.

You say, *loveliness,*
my reply is your name.

That's nice, you say.
It's meant, I say.

You say, *velvet,*
my reply, *your skin.*

You say, *porcelain,*
my reply, *again your skin.*

Velvet porcelain?
That's impossible, you say.

A paradox, I say.

Okay, a hidden lake…
with hills and dales…

Oh, and wooded vales, you say
keeping a straight face.

Shimmering in Paradise? I ask.

Hm..mm, you nod.

Windermere, my dear Sigmund, I say,
making you laugh.

Then I answer true.

That's obsessive, you say,
and so, so rude.

Yes, I say, *you're right.*

Reversion to Type

Other lads wore clogs in school,
other kids were used to clouts,
but my *thee* and *thou* and *sithee*
were singled out by Sir
to shame me in an alien tongue.

I've learned posh language,
can be gentle, tender, speak
not altogether fraudulently
about my love for you.

But sting the Bash-Street kid with scorn
he'll kick your shins with words
as brazen as toe-caps
and from his caulkers
blue strikes detonating.

Henry's Daydream

Who were those ladies encased in crinolines?
His mam's was mute above her bed,
in profile with a parasol,
composed of tarnished silver papers,
smoothed out by a child long gone,
secreted in dark glass and edged
in black with passe-partout.

Aunty Vi's gleams on a Devon toffee tin,
used for buttons and bits of her suspenders.
Only a turned up nose pokes from a hood
but Henry knows the girl blows
pouty kisses to the robins flitting
from the bird-bath to her hand.
She's on tiptoe, one foot raised behind,
innocent of an oo-la-la of petticoats.

Henry daydreams on his Grandma's rug.
In chain-stitch on her fire screen,
a dove-cote and a crazy-paving cottage,
spires of silky hollyhocks
confined behind a picket fence.
A woman reaches out. To try the gate?
Her bonnet hides her face.
Love-birds flutter overhead.

Today, his cataracts float vultures in the clouds,
but the sweet peas Henry grows
make Kate smile straight at him –
better than a thatch-and-lattice box of chocs.
She puts the flowers, not in a woven trug
of golden straw, but in an ice-cream tub,
not dressed in satin, lace and dainty shoes
but T-shirt, tatty jeans and welly-boots.

Henry's Sunday

Henry turns the beef down low,
goes to plant out pansies in the front.

The garden is his peacock's tail.
If Kate looks out today
will she be cheered
to see this irresistible display?

The seeds have ripened on the aconites.
Their yellow cups have been too few.

Henry counts: a year to germinate,
two more to form the tubers
and another two to bud.
He wonders who will live here then,

decides to sow them anyway
even if just for posterity.

He's seen new neighbours
axe hibiscus while they're still in bloom,
lay paving where they grew,
to park the Lexus off the road.

Henry will not modernise,
won't have windows double-glazed

endures the draughts to hear the birds.
Kneeling on the path, he looks up –
after months of winter
Kate's practising a Chopin waltz.

Henry Gardening

It's Sunday in suburbia.
Kate is in the kitchen
basting leg-of-lamb.
Henry's in the great outdoors
digging in the shrubbery.

He shovels snowdrops,
swirls them in the water butt
separating tangled roots.
They wriggle green-tipped silver tails,
swim like sperm beneath a microscope.

Easing apart the mossy lawn
he probes a dibber in the cleft,
pokes in the pearls at just the depth to swell.
Next springtime Kate will see
how they have multiplied.

Kate watches Henry dragging off his boots,
his jumper from his bent grey head,
thinks of ardent afternoons, how they forgot
to fetch the kids from Sunday School –
thought up lies to tell the curate's wife.

While Henry, whistling, washes at the sink
Kate makes *a meal with man-appeal,*
crumbles Oxo in the roasting tin.
Henry thinks she's merely making lunch,
Kate thinks he's just been gardening.

Kate and Henry's Private Garden

You're in the border with a trowel.
Between your jumper and your jeans
the flesh reveals a gleam like silk.
I offer you my garden gloves
to save your hands from sap and thorns.

Now you're away I ring the answer phone.
I have to hear your voice again.
I go into my garden shed,
push my fingers in soft fleece,
warm where yours have been before.

Henry and the Closed Drawer

Henry and Kate curl up in bed
in a comfortable cliché.
He thinks of their silver salad servers
never used in fifty years,
hugging in the baize-lined drawer.
He tries not to think
about curved shapes.
Henry's smiling in the dark.

If only they could die like this –
though no more music,
gardening or poetry,
no more family for goodness sake;
no *Start The Week* or *News Quiz,*
just the drawer shut,
never showing vivid green again.

That might be fine – but at the back
lies the dust of other lives,
creased, faded photos
of the dead, and in the fluff
the clutter of spent matches
hoarded as a boy
when Dad had tried to light his pipe
one windy day.

– horsemen looming pale –

Echo Location

Down a lane I found a gate –
just a gate into a field
and yet, the curlew crying
in an empty sky called on and on.

I tried a hesitant *How do?*
and back it came and came again –
How do? How do? Then silence.

No hand of God had boxed my ears!
I shouted out, *Somebody there?*
heard *'body there? 'body there?*

A decade on I took my sweetheart
on the Sunbeam's pillion seat.
We yelled each other's names,
laughed to hear our names returned.

I roared *I love you!* and
the echo pledged *love you! love you!*

Years afterwards we showed our boys.
Their whoops came bouncing back
Shut up! Shut up!

Today we told our grandchildren
the way to reach the echo gate.
They asked how we discovered it.

Their granny turned her face away.
My first love kissed me there –
he had a motorbike –
but I forget his name – his name.

Bullfinches

Elsewhere, they're shot
for pecking blossom in the bud,
thirty in a minute
till a bough is stripped.

They favour flowers
of a Conference.
If the taste of fruit
is embryonic in the bloom
I think I'd choose it too.

A pair arrived
in early spring, worked
their brazen way along the branches
of our cherry tree.

We traded all that beauty later on
for scarcer beauty now,
fancying the pigment hidden
in the feast
rouged his splendid breast.

One dull morning
he was dead.
We guessed the Sparrowhawk
had caused his crash:
he'd smashed into glass.

His body – soft grey, black, white,
brightest pink and glossy blue –
all buried now
in sunless earth.

Kee, kee – kee, kee,
his widow keened
throughout a week
of wind and rain.
I never saw her feed again.

Begetting

Like mycelia beneath us
the dead are everlasting.
We, the temporarily alive,
are merely fruiting bodies,
toadstools thrust above the substrate,
tender genitals compelled to lust.

We follow coded orders
so their bounds increase,
have to write reports for generals
safe in shelters underground
forever sending out their young
to fight their battles at the front.

We till the earth,
raise crops of wheat and sheep,
build monuments of steel and glass,
invent new words for time and space,
imagine that we've grasped the plot.
The dead have seen it all before.

Below the moss and stones,
their Mafia-embrace of roots
saps all our strength
and feeds us poisoned creeds.
Their blood feuds waste our lives.
To seem both wise and kind
they warn of horsemen looming pale.

We want release from ruthless
greening and decay, but
we are rooted by black apron-strings
and after puffing out our spores,
we deliquesce. What's left of us
the greedy dead suck back
into their mould with glee.

Nor his Ox

Under green fan-vaulted ferns
he glimpses Blue-eyed Mary in the group.
He holds his mossy breath
and longs to open up his anorak,
hop from the ruined hot-house
with her nestled to his chest;
craves to whisper eye-to-eye with her.

He whistles skyward and through curlicues
of russet iron and dagger glass
he hears black rooks
sarcastic in black trees.
In roaring clouds are scraps of Prussian blue
enough for half a pair of trews to fit
this pirate with a wooden leg.

If he robs, his purple wife will scream
more greed than need –
that shoe you nicked from M&S –
wrong style, wrong size, wrong foot,
this is my life and yours you're fucking up –
Their jungle-coloured marriage can allow
no peaceful parallel of lapis-lazuli.

This coveter will go hot-pink, but cool
into the placid lake behind his eyes.
He parrots sombre words in corduroy
like affirmation, empathy and trust.
When women pull his string
they hear a tender teddy-bear,
read *Steiff* within his faux-fur ear.

Made in Hong Kong is printed on his heart,
his New Man manual's in Mandarin.

Larkin' in the Long Grass.

It rained last night.
We rolled the wicket early on,
now steam's rising from the pitch.
I knot my gansey round my bum

and all the world is blue and green
with bits of white that glare like lime –
our togs, the whitewashed hut,
girls' Whitsun dresses breezy-bright.

I'm at deep cover –
the weedy bit beside the tracks
best placed to spot the London trains.

We are only just ahead.
Their only hope is Fatty Dobbs.
Last year the brat made not one run –
our demon-bowler's running up.

I hardly need to watch the match.
I hear the Whitsun Special's snort,
glance to catch its swelling steam
pure above the sooty smoke.

But at a window, a bald head,
black specs looking, looking out;
brown mac in this heat seems sad.
I wave, he does not, the sod.

And then he's gone.

I hear the cheers for Fatty's six –
the howls and groans are all for me
not taking such an easy catch.

Old Misery will never know
how his staring changed the score,
Fatty Dobbs's life, and mine.

Notice

I've seen toadstools
        push through cowpats,
a bird's skull
        bleached by ants,
beetles
        turning turds to soil,
herb robert cling
        to bloomery slag.

I've seen dunlins swarm
        like smoke above the bay,
starlings rise,
        a lava-lamp of sky,
priestly rooks
        enacting rituals before night falls.

I've seen minnows
        with one mind turn silver,
lapis damsel flies
        like Indian beadwork,
meadow browns,
        their wings' dark eyes
like those of a girl
        I'll come to meet.

I've seen lady's mantle's
        cupped green leaves
turn mist to mercury,
        seen difference between
wood and waterside
        forget-me-nots.

I know the drum-roll
        in the dark,
a ceilidh where the scorpions jig
        a-jig, a-jig,
the wailing of a dancing man.

You Are So Sincere

But I am not.
I learnt passion and compassion
two-for-one, from soap opera,
sympathy from Oprah,

empathy from Poundland –
look-alike, smell-alike, feel-alike
new-man stuff
all off a market-stall.

I spoon your self-pity back to you.
You want to think I understand,
let me touch you, move you
with my crocodile symmetric smile.

Yet I am a mammal, horny
corny as a goat,
raging like a caged racoon,
a baboon howling for the moon.

Co-authors of our play,
we know the script –
a lie to live by
while we wait to die.

This human bit's absurd
as mustard in the custard.
So we bray at jackass jokes,
cry like hyenas, you and I.

Earthworks in Edinburgh

Cherries here are still in bud.
Wind chills as I walk towards the gallery,
look up with salty eyes to see Jencks' Earthworks
spiralling across the lawn:

grassy barrows, arcs of water
chafed against the grain by easterlies that scuff the skin
scumble brown clouds
bend bare beeches
shiver grass beneath the tense staves of the fence.

It all might blow away,
a scenic tea towel gusting off the line,
until a swan appears,
anchors the picture to the ground.
His mate gatecrashes, grunting.

There are no sedges here to make a nest.
They take off, thrum with urgency,
circle once the grass below
not seeing anything to suit their purpose
in this harmony of curves.

– the touting ferryman –

Vitrine

Damien Hirst's installation of a shark in a tank of formaldehyde is called 'The Physical Impossibility of Death in the Mind of Someone Living'.

Without a living brain,
can death be imagined?
Where was I before I was born?
my grandson asked.

I tried to explain about
his mother's womb.
But, he said impatiently,
*where was I before **that?***

Nowhere, I thought!
I said, *I don't know* –
couldn't say how easily
each one of us could
have been someone else.

But thinking of a time
before his conception
made it easier to grasp
my own future non-existence.

More help came from Tom,
whose shop is on the square.
He looked up from the counter
and went pale. *I thought
that you were dead,* he said.

I asked, *were many at my funeral?
I bet you didn't go!*
He mumbled how
he was short staffed
deepening the hole he'd dug.

News of the death
of my wife's first husband
lay behind the mistake.
He's the one, I thought,
*who won't be coming
into town again.*

I stepped into the sunny market place
just how it will be when I'm dead –
people going about their business
getting and spending,
not hearing silence from a glass coffin,
hermetically sealed.

Shore Leave with Sirens

At sea he dreams
soft thighs in scarlet skirts,
warm lips whispering.
At anchor in a Boston bar
he hears hot noise to drown in.
He's marooned in camaraderie,
smoke, sweat and scent
cooked-up as carnival.
Sirens whoop inside his head.

I thought that icebergs
lurked behind his eyes
but now I see
the sailor longs for distance,
blue, cold, silent,
to still the menace
milk-eyed Tiresias foretold –
warships blazing black and red,
the smell of seas aflame,
men dying on a rising tide.

After Izzy Orts 1955 by Edward John Burra.

A Day of Life

I'm happy since my brother's death.
Not because his orchid flowers
every spring for me, but for today.

My wife tells me the bath is blocked.
Our visitors are staying overnight.
Soap and hair have choked the outside drain,
black leaves and mud flood on the patio.

It's windy, cold and pouring down.
Whom God loves so He chasteneth.
He times it with slap-stick brilliance.

Sleeve rolled up to shoulder-bone, I plunge
in putrid slime, scrape my flesh.
A delta of bright blood flows down
an arm-length estuary through foul decay.

Never mind – healthier than being dead.
When I've done I shower,
bandage it and have a cup of tea.

Do molecules of stench hang in the brain?
I sniff my skin.
Underneath the shampoo's scent
there is a whiff of carrion.

To Whom do You Talk when
You're Awake in the Night?

I talk to a woman who forgives the sin I can excuse,
and when I'm hot all over for the sin I can't,
says, *well it's not the best thing that you ever did.*
Why clutch at a Judgement Day I don't believe in?

I make up a story of myself – an ordering of chaos,
feelings, absurd associations, all related in word-symbols
no more real than codes for DNA, yet true
as myths and counter myths about the nature of ourselves.

If such a woman remains schtum, like God,
a man will think he's understood.
As others fall for God, he'll fall in love with her,
his ego and himself.

If only we could use each other honestly
as other animals, and accept that we're alone.

In This Interpretation of Events

crows don't roost on high because it's dusk –
they roost to flap their cassocks, caw
the spells and rites that make
the sun go down.
Night, still amethyst, does not fall.
It rises conjured out of corpses,
summoned up from cellars
by the crows.

They spirit it from that portmanteau
hidden underneath a bed -
the bed where you
began by accident
when love, lust and dreams
collided. If not that Friday night,
or Whit Monday, or when big Sis
was at Sunday School –

then you would not be you,
but someone else, someone
from eternal permutations
of the past.
It's odd that you are here at all,
soon to be returned to sender.
You've had a life – a mix of cruelty
and care in your veins.

Don't fear the portent of the crows.
If time's an arrow, not a boomerang,
then it's a lullaby that you can never
not have been.

Waking

I don't believe in ghosts.
Our love will never haunt the ruined church
and warm laughter leaves no echo
on the cold whistle of the sedge.

Our lives are briefer landscapes
in pictures we barely occupy.
They watch us in cruel tolerance
to trap our hopes.

Their images haunt our hearts
as those before and those to come;
show us enough of heaven
to shut the door in our face.

But when you and I are old
I hope to God they let us rest.

The Ultimate Tram

In my teens I stayed in Sheffield where, in 1960, the old trams were being scrapped. The Sheffield Star gave the time and date of the very last tram oddly, though correctly, calling it the Ultimate Tram. The word ultimate was more familiar in describing the latest in manufactured goods after the post-war gloom. For instance my friend's mother coveted a washing machine with a powered mangle advertised as the Ultimate in Home Laundry. So naturally I imagined the ultimate tram as the Acme – the Rolls Royce version. But now I'm getting on there's another connotation.

The ultimate tram is splendid
as a Mississippi riverboat lit up at night,
the upper deck's rococo iron filigree
like balconies on Bourbon Street.

A tramcar named Graves Park
sways and sashays to a G-banjo
as pinstriped minstrels in the bar
croon sweet and low.

They're mirrored in the prisms
of a bevelled glass. Cones of lilies shine
in etched windows with silk curtains,
opulent as fair-ground caravans.

By a gleaming samovar
the white-gloved conductor asks
about my final meal. I can only think
of toasted teacakes.

A jazz band blasts those marching saints.
The silent driver rests his gauntlet
on the big brass handle,
cranks up the town's dead-centre stop.

And off we rock. Wheels in their grooves
swish like a bacon-slicer,
on the points squeal steel on steel
shrill as a blade against a grinding stone.

Paranoia

He has me in his sights.
In the post are catalogues:
commodes, mobility aids,
stair-lifts, incontinence pads.

He knows much more than me –
the worst. I open brochures:
River Cruises down the Rhine,
up the Douro, along the Seine –
ferries accommodating the disabled.

Who needs to go ashore at all?
Last, funeral plans from Age Concern –
apply to-day, save thirty pounds.
Book your Lethe crossing now.

I bin the lot.
The touting ferryman
can whistle for his fare.

Black Letter Days

This Christmas, my love, forget the calendar.
Dates delineated into squares become
black-bordered envelopes for locks of hair.

At each new page, if not this year, I say,
dates bide their time. Will this month be
the month, this day, *the day?*

Long since we sang *Bye bye Miss American Pie,*
windows wound down – somewhere to go,
laughing, *this'll be the day that I die.*

February the twenty-ninth's least likely,
birthdays, the neatest,
cruellest, our anniversary.

Written 19th December 2013, the day he died.

Lightning Source UK Ltd.
Milton Keynes UK
UKHW020932210319
339580UK00007B/25/P